Life with Your Parents

Herman C. Ahrens Jr.

The Pilgrim Press

New York

The scripture quotations are from the Revised Standard Version of
the Bible, copyrighted 1946, 1952, © 1971, 1973 by the Division
of Christian Education of the National Council of the Churches of
Christ in the U.S.A., and are used by permission.

Printed in the United States of America
10 9 8 7 6 5 4 3

This book is printed on acid-free, recycled paper.

ISBN 0-8298-0667-9

The Pilgrim Press, 475 Riverside Drive, New York, NY 10115

To be continued by you . . .

You have control over the person you become. If nature has blessed you, you continue that blessing by the way you take care of the body you have been given. Good posture can be learned, no matter how much your father slouched. Personal hygiene is a self-discipline that makes you healthy, attractive, and full of self-esteem. Bad habits that you unconsciously acquired in early childhood can be consciously changed in late adolescence and in early adulthood. Good habits can be affirmed. And if you are unhappy with the kind of environment in which you grew up, you can rise above it all, if you truly desire. How you use the gifts you have been given will determine the person you are to be.

My parents gave me life at birth. All my physical attributes were formed by their combined genes. In early childhood many of my personality quirks were unconsciously picked up around the home. Later what was happening in the world around me made its impact too. And now my children are adapting to and learning to cope with the bodies their mother and I gave them, the nervous systems we affected, and the world in which they matured. So it is from generation to generation.

The home is still the place where most growing takes place, but now you are more and more on your own. As you move toward your own personhood you build on the best the past has brought to you, you try to understand and learn from what the worst has meant to you, you absorb what is good around you, and you shape it all into the real you that you want to be. And in the process of self-shaping, your life with your parents grows toward a new meaning and maturity.

"You don't understand me!"

In the heat of anger we often say things that have more meaning than we intend at the moment. For example, you shout, "You don't understand me! Nobody understands me!" Just what do you mean? It may be your way of telling your parents, "You won't let me do what I want to do!" But if you are true to yourself and if others are true to you, the understanding you're asking for is much deeper.

For example, you want to be heard in an understanding way by your parents. You want them to listen carefully, weigh answers fairly, and respond squarely. You don't necessarily want your own way, but if you don't get your way, at least you have the satisfaction that you've been heard and that your parents care.

Also you want your parents to understand you as a growing young person—who you really are and what you want to be, what you're going through as you grow, and the pressures you're feeling at home, at school, among your friends.

The you whom you want your parents to understand is a complex human being. But aren't we all? Each of us wants to be treated as a human being for all that means. The humanity we all experience is best nurtured and sustained by adequate food, clothing, shelter, and medical aid in an atmosphere of acceptance and love, with purposeful and caring instruction and conversation and with respect for our personal rights of privacy, fairness, and integrity. Anything less is incomplete. Anything more is a plus for each of us. This is the kind of understanding that's basic to healthy growth and life.

Building trust

"I trust you" is a high compliment.

The best test of strength of character is whether or not you can be trusted. It's natural, then, that you would want to be trusted by your parents. It's normal, then, that building trust starts at home.

Trust starts early in childhood. To the extent that your parents have been affectionate, honest, and supportive, you have grown to trust them. Most parents do not wait until their children are in their teens before they give them opportunities to grow in trust. If you've been taught all through life thus far to tell the truth and you're respected for telling the truth, you've taken the biggest step toward being trusted —not only at home but elsewhere. If you've learned to do what you've promised to do and what you know you're expected to do, you are well on your way to becoming dependable and worthy of trust.

If you think your parents don't trust you, either you have not shown enough evidence to help them feel you can be trusted or your parents have not accurately assessed your ability to be trusted. How can you improve their trust in you? Ask for opportunities to show you can be trusted and don't blow the chances they do give you. For example, if you agree to be home at a certain time, be home at that time, or let your parents know why you're going to be late. If you agree to clean your room by the end of the week, do it. Start with easier responsibilities. As you prove yourself move to more responsible tasks. You should expect your parents to encourage you in your efforts by being trustworthy themselves and by giving you every opportunity to prove your capacity to be trusted. If you want trust, you've got to show trust.

Your problem is not new

The most common error that teenagers with personal problems make is that they feel they are the only person facing their particular problem. They say to themselves, "No one knows what I'm going through because no one else has gone through this before." And so you're hesitant to talk to anyone about your problem, because you feel others won't understand or they might think you're strange. Not so. No matter what your problem, others have gone through it before—probably even your parents when they were younger. It's likely that some young people you know have gone through it before. And so, you are not strange, you are normal; you are not alone, you have company.

The problem itself is not new, but it is new for you. If you're honest with yourself, you would say, "I don't know how to cope with what I'm going through, because I haven't gone through it before." Rather than think something is wrong with yourself or rather than try to go it alone, you turn to those who can help you because they have faced similar problems or because they know persons who have coped with the problem successfully.

Others have answers that can guide you. But more important, others can sympathize with you and can identify with your problems to such an extent that they accept you, not reject you, as you and they together tackle your problem. You will feel as though a load has been lifted off your back when you realize you are not the first to face this problem, that others have coped with it before, and that you are not alone.

Grade A personality

The young student brings home a report card with two Bs, one C, and one D. Most often the parent will say, "How come you got a D?" Not, "Oh, wow! You got two Bs!"

So the young person has a D personality instead of a B personality. The D person feels unappreciated and on the defensive. But the B person has some self-esteem on which to build and is better able to say, "Yes, I got two Bs, but I also got a D and I'll have to work on it."

If yours is the B parent, be thankful.

As human beings, we too often see the bad in a person rather than the good. You cannot build on the bad, but you can build on the good. And there is good in every one of us. Some say the good in each of us is God in us. What is bad, then, is the result of our improperly using God's goodness in us. None of us is perfect in our use of God's gift of goodness. Yet God is the first to forgive us when we err. And God shows us the better way.

Just as you want others to help you build on the goodness that is in you, so you should help others build on the goodness in them. Do you compliment your parents for the good things they do or do you more frequently criticize them for the bad they do? Do you appreciate the good that you do, or are you more likely to put yourself down when you make mistakes? In your attitude toward yourself and toward others are you a B person or a D person? Be one better —be an A person. You deserve it. And so do others.

Love—no matter what!

A parent disciplines a child and the child says, "You don't love me!"

Two parents argue and the child thinks, "Mom and Dad don't love each other anymore!"

It's not that simple.

Love is more powerful than any of us have yet permitted it to be. Love is too big a part of our lives to be trivialized by small understandings. Sure, love can be expressed by hugs and kisses and caresses, kind words and deeds. Love can also be expressed by reprimanding, correcting, and disagreeing. But love is bigger than all these. We can be intelligent, generous, attractive, powerful, religious—but without love we are nothing. With love we can be something. Without love we can achieve nothing meaningful in life. With love life is energized, rewarding and secure.

It is in the home, with the family, that our understanding of love is first nurtured. It is there we first learn to love ourselves, because we are loved. We also learn to give love as well as receive it. If our parents are loving and responsible, we learn to love and to be loved for who we are—no matter what. We learn to dislike our mistakes without disliking ourselves. We want to do what's right out of love, not out of fear. And we learn to dislike the mistakes of others without disliking the persons who make the mistakes. So it is that two people can disagree and still love each other. A parent can discipline a child because love motivates the parent's wanting what is right for the child.

When love hurts

Often young people test their parents' love by seeing how far they can go before the parents withhold love. Such testing is normal. But because a good parent never withholds love from his or her child, a parent can begin to feel a deep hurt when tested unfairly and too long by his or her teenage child. Remember that love is a two-way street—not only from parent to child, but also from child to parent.

Not all people are capable of expressing love in a healthy way. If they don't love themselves (self-esteem), or if they are mentally incapable, or if their nurturing from childhood has never included the establishment of a moral conscience, it is harder—sometimes nearly impossible—for them to know how to love another or receive love. But even when incapable or incompatible, a person sometimes finds that love can break through. Love is a powerful force if truly let free to do its work.

Loving another means that you want what is best for the other. Sometimes "what is best" is not clear to us. For example, when a drunken or desperate father or mother beats or abuses a child—whether teenager or younger—to the point where the child is covered with bruises or where health is threatened, the parent needs help, and those who love the parent will seek help for him or her. Or again, when a child—whether teenager or younger—turns to self-destructive behavior, the child needs help, and those who love the child will seek help for him or her.

Love can hurt and love can heal.

Say it with feelings, not just words

Nothing shapes your life more than your ability to communicate. Your need for food, for affection, and for protection were childhood tests of your getting through to others. You've survived so far. Your needs have now become more sophisticated, so your communication skills must become more sophisticated. How well you learn, develop meaningful relationships, make sense to others, use your talents in work and in play, find your particular niche in the world around you—all depend on how well you communicate. And communication skills are best honed in the family.

A healthy home provides an atmosphere of love, honesty, and mutual respect. Thus, family members spend a lot of time talking with one another. You feel safe to express your feelings. You try to get at the truth. You are counseled when you err. You are credited with "knowing something," even when opinions differ. No rejection. No lectures. You get your conflicts out in the open. You may fight, but you share your thoughts and feelings about dealing with a problem so you can work together toward a solution that is best for everyone.

We're more likely to do what we see than what we're told. We communicate with our total being. Besides words and voice, we "speak" with body language, personal values, past experience, all our senses (sight, hearing, smell, taste, touch), and our storehouse of knowledge. We need to hear the feelings as well as the words. The tone of voice can support or deny the message of our words. And the gentle touch of a hand may mean more than words.

With your ears not your mouth

"Shut up and listen!" an angry parent shouts. The child associates listening with passivity. "You didn't listen to me!" another parent scolds a misbehaving child and the child hears "You didn't obey me!" Listening means obedience. And the child in anger wants to speak. Lesson: Listening does not pay off.

Too often today's society implies that there is power in talking, not in listening. Real understanding takes a beating. Our mouths get in the way of listening.

If you were to jot down some words that best describe a good listener, you might include such adjectives as friendly, open, patient, broad-minded, questioning, honest—a description of a wonderful person. Listening adds to meaningful relationships.

Listening aids good communication. You listen not only with your ears, but with your mind, your heart, your conscience. Enter a conversation to find meaning. Ask questions for clarification. Paraphrase the other's statement to help that person and you know you understand her or his views. Hear corrections and respond accordingly. Listen with attention. Don't let your mind wander so others have to repeat. Don't interrupt. Give honest answers, not flip, phony replies. Agree where you agree, but don't pretend to accept advice you feel is not good. Reassure the other person when you feel the conversation is going well. Don't be judgmental. Be fair. Don't put the other person down. Affirm him or her. Don't criticize personality or character or indulge in name-calling. Stick to the topic.

What if your parents aren't following the same guidelines? One positive listener can turn a shouting match into meaningful dialogue.

Time is tense in our teens

Many young people in their teens cannot imagine life beyond the next five years. What they are experiencing right now is so intense that they cannot believe a parent or another older person who assures them, "You'll outgrow this" or "This is a phase you're passing through."

You probably cannot put into words what's going on within your being, but you sense things are closing in on you. Changes are coming fast. Decisions are becoming more crucial. Expectations are high. Acceptance by others is vital.

Will you ever get through it all?

Yes! But you won't believe that now. So you have to have faith and trust and confidence. And before you know it, time will cause you to look back and to wonder, "What was all the worry about?" And you'll start counseling those who are younger than you, "Don't worry so much. This too will pass."

Within a span of eight years, for example, your perspective on life and on your understanding of your relationship with your parents can change considerably. Take the testimony of one who passed this way before you. At twelve, she tells her parents, "Let me do it myself. Give me a chance." At sixteen, she says, "I don't need you. I can think for myself and I know where I'm going." At eighteen, she says, "Let me be free to live. I want to be on my own." Then, at twenty, she writes home: "I am a child in a new sort of way. You are my special friends. I love you and I need you to love me. You have given me life and the means by which to live it. You know me better than anyone and yet you still love me."

The screen is scrambled

You watch an R-rated movie on cable TV. Your parents scold you. You don't understand. They say you shouldn't watch such movies, that they're bad for you. Why? You'll get the wrong ideas about sex. You still don't understand. All the kids you know talked about the movie. What's all the fuss?

Sometimes the media sends mixed messages. What you see on TV is not always the way you live life in your home. So your parents are probably concerned. You are viewing real-life situations that your parents feel you might not be mature enough or informed enough to handle appropriately. Are you learning too much too fast? Are you able to integrate all this into a healthy life-style? Your parents fear for you. Their concern is even more serious if, in their own minds, they're not sure themselves how to handle this dilemma.

You are a child of a new age. You were born into a world of hi tech, nuclear power, space exploration, computers, and home electronic entertainment. For many, these advances have complicated life, especially moral decisions.

This complication is being passed on to you and to others your age. Your generation bears the burden of working through this confusion to some sort of resolution. You are being subjected to making decisions for which you're not completely programmed. You have no precedents against which to measure yourself. You have no new-age models to follow. You have to set your own path.

When parents split

It's tough on kids when two parents disagree with each other. It's tougher still for everyone when parents have tried hard to make things work out but decide "it is better for two people to be happy living apart rather than be unhappy living together."

A single-parent family or a stepfamily or a reorganized family needs to be recognized for its unique characteristics. In this situation, children very much want meaningful relationships—love and acceptance from their parents and for their parents, as well as respect for their own personal integrity.

When parents decide to separate, the children have no choice in the decision. Certainly they don't want to be blamed by the parents for something over which they have no control. But the children want to be assured by the parents that they won't be deserted in the process. They resent one parent trying to turn the children against the other parent.

At your age, a family split may demand of you new responsibilities. As a young adult, you are mature enough to be an advocate for your brothers and sisters and to be a good listener, a comfort, and a conscience to your parents.

A split in the family will expose you to extra social pressures, to unsavory facts of life, and to new depths of initiative you never knew you had. Your faith will be tested and probably enriched. Your ability to love people while not agreeing with them will be strengthened. The healing power of love may take on new meaning. Although you and your parents may never be together again as a family, your love may be the medicine that soothes, even heals, the hurts in your own life as well as the hurts in the lives of others.

You'll never walk alone

Most of the problems you face can be resolved through honest and open discussion with your parents. But what if you feel you've exhausted every possible way to work through a problem at home? You turn to the support system outside your home.

"Where do I turn?" you ask. "Who will listen to me —really hear me out? Who can be trusted to keep a confidence? Who knows what they're talking about? Who will ask decisive questions to guide me in thinking through my confusion? Who will care enough to correct me but not condemn me? Who will support me but not exploit me?"

The degree of seriousness and confidentiality of your problem will determine to whom you should talk—a mature adult you respect, a relative, a trusted neighbor or friend, a teacher, a minister, a doctor, a lawyer, a professional counselor. Ask others, "Who is a good person with whom I can talk?" Would they introduce you?

A word of caution: In times of desperation and confusion some people look for easy and quick solutions or are lured into relationships they would not normally approve for themselves, or they put aside their fine facilities for critical questioning and for maintaining their high values. When they are hurting, they are easy prey for the uninformed, the immature, the suave persuaders, the exploiters, even the crazies. Such possibilities only add to their uncertainty.

Many people out there really care, but sometimes we don't find them until we need them and look for them.

Put away childish ideas

"I don't believe in God anymore," says the teenager. Is it an excuse not to go to church? Is it your way of saying you're growing up? Is it a confession that you've hit a stone wall in your personal search for a power beyond yourself? It's probably all three. But none of these answers faces the reality of God in your life.

As people grow older they find their idea of God that satisfied them as children is inadequate. That doesn't mean there isn't a God anymore. More likely it means their idea of God is not big enough now to meet the demands of their more mature outlook on life. Many adults are nonbelievers today because in their teens and twenties they made no effort to develop a more adequate concept of God, one that would satisfy their growing minds and spirits.

In the midst of your search for a bigger understanding of God it is self-defeating to stop going to church. The church is the one place in society where you should be able to grow in your understanding of God and of yourself. If the church has not helped you, maybe it's because you have not pressed the church to answer your more mature probings about God, about faith, and about life's ultimate questions. If you find the church inadequate in its witness, you should stay and challenge it. When you leave the church everyone suffers.

Whatever you do in your spiritual search, give it time. In fact, it may take the rest of your life to sharpen a living concept of God that is to be your conscience, your comfort, and your light for that more mature and more complete person you are becoming.

When i'm in doubt

I'm not sure about a lot of things. For starters, I'm not sure about who I am, where I'm going with my life, what love is all about, or whether there's a God. Yet somehow I feel all these things are tied together.

Despite what others say, I feel there's nothing wrong with doubting or asking questions. It's my way of searching for answers—the right answers for me. There's so much to find out about life, about myself, about everything. It's both exciting and scary! Friends and family and teachers try to help. But there seems to be that certain something that no one else can quite give to me—a wisdom, a compassion, a purpose, a power that is alive in that fertile vastness of my mind and my spirit.

Is that you, God? I hope so! I need you in a way I've never needed you before. Be with me, God.

Surrendering to Someone

I don't know who—or what—put the question. I don't know when it was put. I don't even remember answering. But at some moment I did answer "Yes" to Someone or something. And from that hour I was certain that existence is meaningful and that, therefore, my life, in self-surrender, had a goal.

—Dag Hammarskjöld

Running the good race

Therefore, since we are surrounded by so great a cloud of witnesses, let us also lay aside every weight, and sin which clings so closely, and let us run with perseverance the race that is set before us.

—Hebrews 12:1

When i've made a mistake

Everybody is acting as if I did it on purpose. But it was an honest mistake. I misjudged. I was awkward. I was naive. I was uninformed. But everyone else acts as if I'll never grow up. That's the point! My mistake was caused by what I did not know. Now I know. And that's how I grow.

Why do we ridicule people who make mistakes? How can we tell the difference between people who make mistakes just to be doing something wrong and people who make mistakes because they don't know any better?

Thank you, God, for parents who understand that we grow by each new experience. They are there to comfort us when we fail and affirm us when we succeed. They know when we are really trying. And so do you, God.

The space inbetween

If you have built castles in the air, your work need not be lost; that is where they should be. Now put the foundations under them.   —Henry David Thoreau

Maturing by wisdom

Any person can make mistakes, but only an idiot persists in that error.   —Cicero

It's bigger than both of us

As you did it to one of the least of these my brethren, you did it to me.   —Matthew 25:40

When i'm right

I know I'm right, dear God. But my parents won't admit it. It's been several days since we first disagreed. Now time has proven me right. Friends of the family have assured me I'm right. But my parents act as if it's just a small thing and they won't tell me that I'm right or that they're wrong. But several days ago this was a big thing to them. Now it's a big thing to me.

I'm not really angry with them, but I am disappointed. They've taught me to be honest and reconciling when I know I'm wrong. But they also say I should stand firm, yet be affirming when I learn I'm right.

Dear God, it's not a matter of who won or who lost, or who's right or who's wrong. It's a matter of behavior, of attitude, and of understanding. Help us all to do the right that parents have taught us to do. Amen.

A little and a big thing

Regard it as just as desirable to build a chicken house as to build a cathedral. The size of the project means little in art, beyond the money matter. It is the quality of character that really counts. Character may be large in the little or little in the large.

—Frank Lloyd Wright

A big boy now

When I was a child, I spoke like a child, I thought as a child, I reasoned like a child; when I became a man, I gave up childish ways.   —1 Corinthians 13:11

When they say i'm too young

My parents treat me like a child. They don't seem to realize I'm growing up. My body is maturing. I've got a mind of my own. I can take care of myself. I know more about life than my parents think I do. Don't they trust me?

But I'm old enough to wonder: Am I trying to be older than I am? Is my body growing faster than my mind and soul can manage? Do I have the wisdom to make the most of my new knowledge? Am I ready to cope with life situations I've never faced before? Do my parents know things about life I might do well to heed? Do they love me more than I know?

Dear God, I need to reach out to be more than I was but not more than I'm capable of being. My parents are hesitant and I am eager. Temper my eagerness with my own deeper desire to do what is right for myself and for others. Ease their uncertainty with their own confidence in what they have taught me through the years. Amen.

Always growing

When I was a boy of 14, my father was so ignorant I could hardly stand to have the old man around. But when I got to be 21, I was astonished at how much he had learned in seven years. —Mark Twain

Fruit of the vine

For the moment all discipline seems painful rather than pleasant; later it yields the peaceful fruit of righteousness to those who have been trained by it.
—Hebrews 12:11

When i want to say "i love you"

Sometimes I'm hard on my parents and then when I want to tell them I'm sorry, I don't know how.

Sometimes I feel good about myself and I want to share my enthusiasm with others, but will they think I'm too self-centered?

Sometimes I'm really proud of my father, but he's so shy about my showing any affection, either by my loving words or by my touching him.

Dear God, your love has set all creation into being. You have made love the heartbeat of all relationships. Your way of love is so natural, yet we have made it seem unnatural. Help us to love with the honesty you meant us to love. Amen.

Reach out and touch . . .

Just because the message may never be received does not mean it is not worth sending.   —Segaki

Confessions of a saint

If you love me, let it appear.   —St. Augustine

And the greatest of these . . .

Love is patient and kind; love is not jealous or boastful; it is not arrogant or rude. Love does not insist on its own way; it is not irritable or resentful; it does not rejoice at wrong, but rejoices in the right. Love bears all things, . . . endures all things.

—1 Corinthians 13:4-7

When i don't know what to do

I know there's an answer for my question, a solution for my confusion, a light for my darkness. I have confidence in the future, if I can only get past my present dilemma. Help me, God.

Help me pinpoint my problem. Help me put aside the surface issues and get to the heart of the matter. Help me be honest in mind, spirit, and body. Give me strength to handle the hardships my searching causes. Give me courage to do what is right in your sight.

Clean my mind of destructive, hateful, and negative solutions. These are not your ways, O God. Fill me with your ways of creative, caring, and positive solutions. Your ways are not easy, God, but I know your ways are right for me.

I am not alone. Even though I sometimes wonder if anyone really cares, I know there is support, counsel, and help, only if I really try. My parents want to help. Other family members and friends care. There is also my pastor, a special teacher, a caring doctor, a respected counselor.

But, God, do not let me turn in my desperation to those who will exploit or hurt me.

And I am thankful that while I'm searching I have you, God, to comfort me and guide me. Amen.

One step at a time
Nothing is particularly hard if you divide it into small jobs.   —Henry Ford

Go for it
And whatever you ask in prayer, you will receive, if you have faith.   —Matthew 21:22

When i retreat to my room

I just have to get away from it all. Sometimes I'm angry and need to cool off. Sometimes I'm confused and need to think by myself. Sometimes I feel pushed and need to back off. But never when I go to a place all alone—in my room, to a favorite quiet spot, or for a walk—am I running away. I know I must eventually learn to channel my emotions, clarify my thinking, and handle the pressures I face.

When I'm alone, dear God, I feel your presence more than at any other time. Sometimes it's scary. Then I realize I shouldn't be afraid of you. Maybe it's the weight of my feeling and thinking and doing on my own that scares me. I have to sift everything through myself. When I leave my retreat I feel refreshed, relaxed, ready to go again. Thanks, God. Amen.

Take time to be whole

We have all this beauty around us and yet grownups often forget about it. I hope that you will be more sensible and open your eyes and ears to this beauty and life that surround you. As young people, you play and work with one another and it is only when you grow up that you begin to learn about barriers from your elders. Young people, I hope you will take a long time growing up.   —Jawaharal Nehru

You never walk alone

You shall love God with all your heart, and with all your soul, and with all your strength, and with all your mind; and your neighbor as yourself.
                              —Matthew 22:37-39 (adapted)

When all is well in my family

It was a great day! I didn't get angry when I was called earlier than usual this morning. Breakfast was tops! At school I got a good grade on an exam in my hardest class. After school I rushed home from practice to do my chores. When I went off on a date tonight Mom lectured me as usual on how to behave, but I understood. After my date I thanked my folks for not scolding me when I was several minutes past my curfew deadline. And I was complimented for phoning home when I knew I was going to be late. I'll sleep well tonight.

Thanks, God, for those times when we can enjoy the results of harmony at home, caring family members, behavior taught by example, obedience that we want to do, good food, healthy exercise, stretching of mind and spirit, and sufficient rest to stimulate the juices of our being. May we never forget the good things that living in a family has brought to each of us. As we someday become parents, may the best of what we have experienced in our homes be passed on to our own children. Amen.

Peace be with you

Have no anxiety about anything, but in everything by prayer and supplication with thanksgiving let your requests be made known to God. And the peace of God, which passes all understanding, will keep your hearts and your minds in Christ Jesus.

—Philippians 4:6-7